july 23   august 23

leo

WHITE STAR PUBLISHERS

contents

Text by
Patrizia Troni

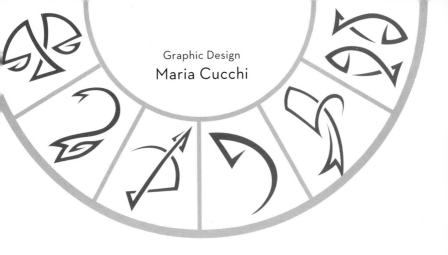

Graphic Design
Maria Cucchi

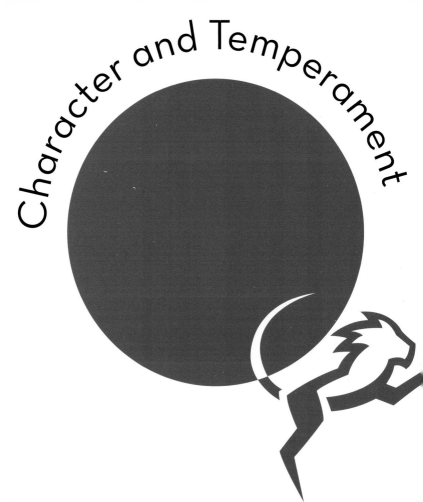

Character and Temperament

Sunny, explosive and self-assured, Leos can easily be considered the Zodiac sign with the biggest ego of all. With them, it would seem that humans have something divine about them, given that they are certain that they are perfect. This self-confidence is translated into power and domination that has its positive and negative traits.

They are positive because believing in oneself, in one's strength, is fundamental in life thanks to their great store of energy, which, although it needs long periods of rest to recuperate fully, could be called inexhaustible. They are negative because the world often challenges the great self-assurance they parade, and this might

end up isolating them. And, while their pride prevents them from exhibiting how much they suffer from this, it is also true that it is their typical individualism that sometimes leads them to become isolated and to have to proceed alone, like heroes of ancient times.

Leos are, and always want to be, totally independent. They believe, first and foremost, in themselves with the great vitality and confidence that supports them on every occasion. Strong, self-assured, domineering and exuberant, they openly and fearlessly reveal what they are, so much so that at times they exaggerate and become too bold and courageous.

Leos are convinced that they are the best and always give the best of themselves, they love doing their best and always demand the best and most of others. No one can be better than them or dominate them; they don't want to ask anything of anyone or depend on anyone. And, at certain moments, rather than frightening them, solitude excites and stimulates them even more. Vigorous, luminous and galvanizing, they are the captain, the director, or better, the general who gives orders and leads, certain of their power, endowed as they are with determination coupled with great ambition. The world often follows them; others rely on them, applaud and praise them, creating a driving force that leads them to reach for even higher objectives, because there is nothing they feel unable to achieve.

Such vitality also offers them the pleasure of self-satisfying performance that is increasingly enhanced as they attain results and victories. They like to take center stage, be spectacular and attract everyone's attention. For them 'grandeur' is not a fault but rather a natural condition, and they show this off with a nonchalance that makes them even more likeable, admired and desired. Grandiose achievement is much more to their taste than a comfortable, convenient and dull routine, the nondescript mediocrity of an average, obscure everyday life.

Leos thirst for the sensational, they like to feel important, they are not afraid of strenuous effort. They proceed with their head held high to shoulder all kinds of responsibility, and others follow them because they have a big heart, which is expressed in their unstinted generosity. Leos are magnanimous and do their utmost for others; they surpass themselves thanks to the energy and power they always emanate.

Leos certainly do not suffer from the illness of self-criticism and they have no intention of being entangled in underrating themselves. On the contrary, they tend to overrate themselves. Leos proceed without complicated tactics or strategies; they are warm, direct, open and especially influential and dominating. They are the leader, the guide, the CEO. They can be a little bit narcissistic, with a dash of haughtiness as well as touchiness, always with pride and boldness that makes them think they have the right to feel superior.

Love and Passion

8 Leo

In matters of love, Leos also like to transcend limits and create their own rules. Passion for them is fire, incandescence that suddenly explodes and overwhelms both them and everything around them. Leos are a sunny and fantastic image that everyone must admire, and when passion is sparked then the object of that love must be theirs immediately. Their great store of desire will not admit of half measures or roundabout behavior. When they want something or someone, they want it right away. And, when the object of their love is finally theirs, he or she can then indulge fully in their generosity. They give their all in matters of love, and, at the same time, expect to be everything to their partner. While it is true that Leos are the center of the universe that illuminates and creates life, those they love must treat them for what they are – objects of adoration, gods and goddesses who, if loved and worshipped, in turn bestow absolute passion and generosity on the person they love. Leos are sincere and loyal when they manifest their affection, without ever wanting to be questioned or contradicted, since for them there is no doubt in love. Once the Sun is high in the sky and warms the entire globe, there is no reason to cover it with clouds of uncertainty. When they love, they do not want complications. They dislike tortuosity and ambiguity. Leos represent the pleasure of giving and giving of

themselves, and their image must shine like something everyone can see and desire. When they are in love they give everything they have. When their passion is aroused, no one can compete with them. Leos are the world's experts in courtship; they regale the person they love with attention, kindness, and other signs of affection both large and small that make their partner feel desired to the utmost.

Leos are overwhelming in lovemaking. They do not spare themselves and do not conceal their real feelings behind cold inhibition. They are not afraid of excess. They are felines that capture their prey and make it theirs.

When love then takes on a stable dimension, they also know how to lapse into a state of tranquility in which their partner must show that he or she is able to be in tune with Leo's lazier, more indolent ways. Because the red hot sun of desire, which, when it is at its zenith, burns like nothing else, certainly cannot remain at its zenith for ever and must, therefore, indulge in its sweet, relaxing and comfortable twilight. But, their night of love will be long lasting. The ardor of desire soon returns inexorably and then the entire universe once again begins to burn with boundless and unbridled love.

In love, as in life, Leos want to be unique, the only ones. And, they know they are unique. They are too grand to display those all-too-human defects of jealousy and possessiveness. No rival must be in their vicinity. The logic of competition, suspicion and doubt is foreign to Leos because Leos consider themselves winners from the outset.

Should their partner stop making them the center of attention and the most important thing on earth, something fades away inside them. As proud as they are, they can bear this in silence and do not show their feelings, but if the ardent passion turns into lukewarm affection, they do suffer. Just as love for them means wholly giving of themselves, so there must not be anything cold, gelid or calculated in their partner's behavior.

Consequently, while Leos fight like invincible beasts in order to win a person's heart, if they then must vie with a potential rival they prefer to back off and seek love elsewhere – not because they are cowardly or afraid of conflict, but simply because their regal, absolutist nature will not acknowledge that two suns, theirs and that of their rival, can illuminate the relationship. No one can take their place. They are kings and queens and must reign supreme in the heart of the one they love.

How to Hook a Leo and How to Let Them Go

In the world of nature, it is the lioness that hunts, while the male arrives when the prey is ready to be eaten. In astrology, as well the female Leo is more seductive, resolute and determined in courtship. If attracted, she is the one who takes the initiative, displaying generous passion that gives its all and loves unrestrainedly. The 'lioness' is the very essence of the power of love. She is not the right person for men who are indecisive, wavering or ill at ease. She wants, by her side, a self-assured, strong man, preferably important and socially in the public eye, a man who supports her in everything and has her constantly in his thoughts while at the same time accepting her independence. In order to win her heart you should tell her that you were dazzled by her from the first moment and that there is no other woman in the world like her. Another suggestion: take her to smart, stylish places, make her feel she is the best, the most beautiful and desirable.

The male Leo is a bit lazier, or perhaps only prouder, than his counterpart during courtship. He does want to reveal his feelings and his attraction for the woman. He prefers not to commit himself until he is sure of success, partly because a possible rejection would be a blow that would be difficult to recover from. Leos are bad losers. Rather than hear her refuse him, he puts off courtship and studies his 'prey', and should the conquest be too difficult he will look elsewhere. For him, courtship can be prolonged a little, but when sparked by passion there can be no hesitation. If the spark flares, he goes all the way. In order to hook him you must listen to him as if enchanted, and not be too docile or too standoffish. Be presentable at all times. If you bring him coffee in bed, you will make him feel he's a true king. If you want to end the relationship, bear in mind that he or she appreciates frankness and a quick break-up. It is better to state clearly that the love story is over and leave in peace. Leos want to lick their wounds in solitude.

Compatibility with Other Signs

It is very easy to establish who is compatible with Leos. They are the people who adore them, love them with all their heart, and place them on a pedestal as the only person worthy of being loved. However, sometimes their strong character needs someone who is able to cope with them and at the same time can trigger immediate sympathy and accord, a magical harmony of the senses and vitality in which their energy explodes in unison in the direction of enthusiastic love. The like-mindedness with Aries is simply splendid and becomes more receptive to the world of knowledge and adventure in a relationship with Sagittarius. Leos get along famously with Geminis because they know how to please them and sound the right note at the right moment. Their excellent compatibility with Libras is more aesthetic, refined and formal. Leo-Taurus couples do exist, although the essential nature of the first sign of Earth is too pragmatic and simple and consequently does not provide them with the flashes of exuberance that they need. Coupling with Cancers is magnificent and frequent as well, since those born under that sign unconsciously love being protected by their prodigious power. Great love stories can take place between Leos, but their limit lies in the dispute over which of the two is in command: the king may want the queen, but the queen certainly has no intention of succumbing to the king. Their nature agrees to quite a degree with that of Virgos, whose intelligence they appreciate very much. They have a strong attraction for Scorpios, but the relationship often becomes complicated because their character is too mysterious and contorted for their sunny disposition. With a Capricorn, they can work together on a professional level, but this is by no means the sign that takes them to seventh heaven with a thousand compliments: in other words, it is a relationship with its ups and downs. Transgressive attraction and interesting friendships can be established with Aquarius, although the connection does not always prove to be long lasting and suitable. Pisces fascinate them a lot, but they do not always sympathize with their contradictory nature and fragility.

Leo Profession and Career

Leo's independent and extreme individualist nature is expressed quite well in their profession. Whatever they undertake, they like to do it by themselves, just as they like to make all the decisions and assume all the responsibility that this entails. A dull job in an out-of-the-way and undistinguished context is what they refuse more than any other. Even when they are an employee, feeling important and indispensable is fundamental. They must demonstrate to themselves and to the entire world that they are able to solve problems, take the initiative, successfully conclude negotiations and bargaining, create something wholly new that is superior in quality to everything else ever seen previously in a company or a commercial context. The need to feel rewarded and admired for what they do is the motor that gives meaning to their activity. It is very important to remind their superiors that they can never treat Leos like just another employee of the firm, with a job consisting of banal duties or dull routine. Having the security of a permanent job does not satisfy Leo; what does is the sensation of being central, essential, one of the spearheads of the firm. Leo's superior must tell them clearly that they are doing quite well, that they

are important and irreplaceable for the attainment of great goals. If this satisfaction exists then Leos are eager to give their all, achieving objectives that are even greater than what was expected.

If, on the other hand, Leo is a manager or entrepreneur, they are very generous with those under them, offering understanding and help, but their authority must be acknowledged and respected because objections to, and lack of recognition of, their role makes them lose their patience. They need capable collaborators, reliable, intelligent and loyal people. Attracting rivalry is in the DNA of a Leo: subtle envy that causes their colleagues to work against them, often without their realizing this. Leo's self-assurance and generosity also contains a good dose of ingenuousness.

In general, Leos can achieve excellent, even sensational, results the more they tend to be proud of themselves and to surpass themselves, while in periods of crisis, slowdown or negative results they tend to become too discouraged, which sometimes aggravates the situation. Leos were born to triumph and they dislike unsatisfactory

✿　　✿　　✿　　✿　　✿　　✿　　✿

results and detest the taste of failure. They are ambitious creatures and this ambition is not to be confused with vanity. When Leos have a goal in mind they find all the determination and combativeness they need, which go well beyond methodical procedure. They do not have the spirit of an office employee who is satisfied with his routine daily tasks. They like exploits. They are not suitable for unremarkable teamwork, but, if they do work in a team, their leader personality will emerge at a certain point, and, if they really believe in this, their spirit becomes contagious and they transmit their enthusiasm and doggedness to the other team members.

Leos are also fine teachers. They do not keep their knowledge to themselves but, with their typical generosity, transmit it to others. Many Leos are high school teachers, company managers and even professional figures connected to chief executive officers who end up running the firm. Due to the connection that Leo has with nightlife, many Leos are disc jockeys, disco and nightclub managers and owners, astronomers and night watchmen.

How Leo Thinks and Reasons

Most Leos do not waste time having daydreams and vague thoughts that lead to nothing concrete. They adore the obvious, clear, luminous truth and precise, well-defined thoughts. They may, occasionally, be slightly off the mark as regards the accuracy of certain details, but they always go to the heart of the matter right away, without the slightest hesitation.

Sometimes their reasoning, like the process of an equation, skips over or fails to pay proper attention to necessary passages because they are not accountants, but passionate visionaries convinced that they are depositories of the truth. However, this does not mean that they are superficial: their proud, loyal spirit, which they manifest in the various circumstances of life, and also in thought, without any desire to deceive.

True, at times, their thought verges on narcissism and exhibitionism. It may happen that they like to listen to themselves talk and, at times, they enjoy saying something amazing and spectacular. Leos alternate brief and dry essentiality with colorful and warm conversation rich in details. But, they never lose sight of the crux of the matter and, when the right moment comes, they vigorously say what they really think, without being particularly diplomatic. Leos alternate moments of humility and meditative silence with others in which it seems that they have been illuminated by a divine spark, when their mind becomes a torrential flow of dazzling ideas. When they want to express an objective or a thought, rarely is it something mediocre presented in a simple way. They like to think big, aim at goals that transcend the confines of the sky. For them the impossible must never be impossible.

In general, Leos are not trapped in the obscure labyrinth of contorted reflection. For them, thought is sheer pleasure and must never become torture. If there is a problem to be solved that drags on, Leos always manage to find the answer with one blow.

It may be there are people whose intelligence is more critical, prompt and precise than theirs, but their thought process is never a cold task that must be carried out according to predictable canons. They enjoy amazing and surprising their questioners, catching them off guard, showing them that truth is always exciting and goes hand in hand with great vitality and energy. Few people are as fond of pure abstraction as Leo is, just as they are not at all interested in or attracted by arid and pragmatic realism. Their mind, like their personality, has something unique and heroic about it that distinguishes it from the commonplace and trite.

Another characteristic of their intelligence, which is also a virtue, is that they do not separate their thought from their heart and instinct. When their process of reasoning is described as warm, instinctive and immediate, this means that they are not one of those people who isolate reason from passion, making them inaccessible from one another and perhaps even casting one of them into the oblivion of their unconscious. However, this is not to say that Leos provide others with reasoning contaminated by sentimentalism and confused by emotion. In general, when Leos talk, they much prefer to have an audience; the larger it is, the more exciting it becomes for them. Although Leos do quite well when they are alone, and not depending on anyone else is essential for them, it is undoubtedly a great feeling when others applaud and praise them. The larger their audience, the better they give of themselves. When the king of the forest speaks, all the crocodiles, hippopotami, parrots and giraffes listen to him in silence, since something important and enlightening is about to be announced.

Sociability, Communicatio

nd Friendship

Leos are independent and are used to relying solely on themselves. At the same time, however, they also have a sociable and communicative character. They are quite happy to be alone, and having to deal with something when left to their own devices is no problem for them. But, this does not mean that they do not enjoy being in company, especially when they are the guiding light, the beacon, of the group.

Leos do not depend on sociability; they do not mingle with other people because their life would have no meaning without them. The world does not attract them like a magnet or condition them, yet they certainly appreciate and enjoy the flurry of society. And, when others appreciate and acknowledge their many qualities then they are even happier, exuberant and excited. A large circle of people revolves about them, old and new friends; and like a king in his court, on the one hand they dispense the light and strength of their personality, and on the other hand receive, in exchange, confirmation that they are truly unique and special individuals.

This magnetic power of theirs is clearly visible in friendship, where they often give more than they receive. In their social relationships, they are not opportunistic, egoistic, or pretentious; they never lean on others but offer their support willingly. With their friends, they are the ones who take the lead and are at the helm. Fragile and insecure people can rely totally on their strength. They never refuse to help. They have the sense of giving to others, they like to offer advice and suggestions, and they feel good when they propose the best solution to a problem. Supporting and helping a friend warms their heart.

When in company Leos like to make a sensation. Often they are a fine conversationalist, brilliant and expansive, always with something spectacular to display or transmit. Their sense of hospitality, their capacity to prepare an ideal situation or setting for those who are arriving, are impressive, even though this might entail going beyond their means.

In every relationship, whether it concerns business, friendship or love, they demonstrate total loyalty and honesty, without any trace of pettiness.

Where true friendship is concerned, when they really cherish their relationship with someone, they spare no efforts, even becoming heroic, with the devotion and helpfulness of a person who reaches extraordinary levels of altruism. The above-mentioned virtues of loyalty, clear-cut sincerity and honesty – which leads others to forgive their minor shortcomings of narcissism and egocentricity that sometimes crop up – emerge in friendship as well. True, they do not like to be contradicted and find it difficult to apologize. It is also true that in a conversation they use the first person singular quite often, but this strongly accentuated 'I' is always sincerely and truly at the disposal of other persons, who understand and appreciate this.

On a social level, this 'overexposure' in behavior and communication might end up triggering some form of envy or jealousy. This could irritate them, but usually not only do they ignore such feelings, they don't even notice them. Leos try to see only the best side of other persons. Should someone glower at them or criticize them maliciously, this does not challenge their vision of reality in the least. They continue to be themselves utterly.

When Leo Gets Angry

It's quite easy to make Leos angry. One need only admit that they are not always right and not flatter them. Part of the Leo DNA consists of the conviction of being the best by divine right. If others do not acknowledge this and contradict them, this is high treason in their opinion. The Sun in their sign strengthens the centrality of a regal 'I'. Those not born under Leo must be their respectful subjects, not impertinent antagonists.

Lions and lionesses love staying in the shade of a baobab and attack only if they must find food or if someone tries to pull their tail. Likewise, Leos do not attack if there is no good reason to do so. They are not irascible troublemakers, but if others offend their self-respect, if they challenge their charisma, their words and decisions, then they look them straight in the eye, bare their teeth and give them a blow with their powerful paw.

If there is a dispute Leos don't waste any time, but get right to the point, without unfair blows or half measures. Keeping things in abeyance is not for them. Should there be the least suspicion or misunderstanding they want to clarify it right away, not dwell in doubt or postpone an explanation. Leo is light, and light needs transparency and clarity. Pride, which is their Achilles heel, and their tendency to command and impose their will, make it almost impossible for them to accept someone's telling them what to do and not to do without a reaction on their part. Whoever tries to impose their will on Leo is running a risk. Leos want everything, and immediately, which means that they expect their every wish to be granted and their orders to be complied with right away. Those who disappoint Leo, stall for time, do not keep a promise, not only make them angry but must also make quite an effort to regain their respect. Leo may be arrogant and proud, but harboring resentment is not part of their character. They may even get angry, but if those who hurt them offer an explanation with sincere feeling, they are only too willing to pardon them.

Leo Children

Just as an adult Leo wants to be in the center of the world, the lion cub wants to be in the center of the family (universe), the Sun around which attention and affection revolve. Sensitive to compliments and craving approval and consideration, these children do not want to be small but to be considered adults in an adult world. And, if the latter, the parents and teachers, know how to inspire respect and admiration in the children and provide them with warmth, vivaciousness and stimuli, they will find it easy to be obeyed and loved.

Given their innate pride, it is advisable not to scold them in front of strangers and to try to control and tame their exuberant nature without reprimanding and punishing them too much. The education of these children must be a delicate process, never too severe or rigid. Nor should parents or teachers be too permissive, because should the lion cubs' relatives be weak and forbearing, the youngsters will very soon become despots that tyrannize everyone around them. You must be patient and firm with them, speak to their heart. Sermons and scoldings are useless with these cubs. The mere sight of their sad mother and upset father makes them immediately regret what they did.

These vivacious, sunny, smiling children find it easy to make friends but are also quite content to play by themselves. And, in their circle, they are naturally the leaders, the playmates that the others follow in their games and other activities. If the group

gets into mischief, Leos are the first to take the blame to save their friends. This is their heroic side, their capacity to sacrifice themselves for others. While Leos have a good dose of presumptuous pride from an early age, there is also a basic humility that prompts them to understand and help others, which they do with all their heart.

Music Associated

In the field of music, Leos are spectacular and overwhelming protagonists. The undisputed prototype is Mick Jagger, with all his magnetic energy, which sustains a powerful rhythm, and that gift of always managing to be in the limelight, regaling all his fans with pulsating, vital music that is the exact opposite of the delicate, ironic atmosphere created by the Beatles, the great rivals of the Rolling Stones. Although music, for Leos, has its moments of sublime and magical poetry, the essence of its character is to transmit the all-powerful surge of life. This is also true in the case of leading figures and pioneers in the history of jazz, such as that famous Leo, Louis Armstrong, the undisputed master of 1920s and 1930s jazz. There are not many Leos who were or are great classical musicians; it is as if only in jazz, rock, ska or reggae does this sign of Fire succeed in giving the best of itself. However, typical Leo audacity and courage are often present with extraordinary innovators, for example, the contemporary Ger-

with Leo

man composer Karlheinz Stockhausen. Leo's regality is part and parcel of symphony orchestra conductors, such as one of the leading ones of our day, Riccardo Muti. As for female Leos who have made their mark in music, the strong personality and ability to hold an audience are quite noticeable in Madonna, the classical innovative and scene-stealing lioness whose extraordinary personality is a fundamental ingredient of her musical production. But, the same holds true for other Leo women with great class, for example Kate Bush and Jennifer Lopez. Typically, Leo music is also performed by the rocker from Indianapolis, John Hiatt, whose warm, engrossing music combines the power of Leo's Fire sign with a great deal of harsh and virile lyricism that goes straight to one's heart.

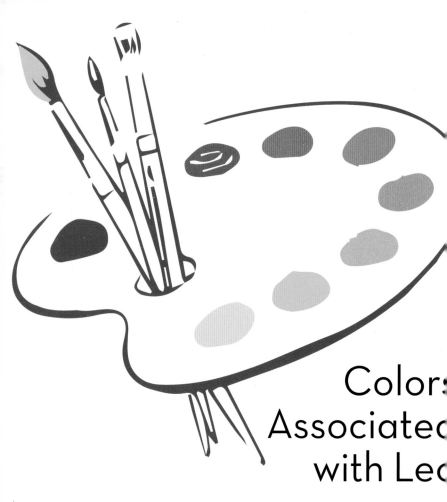

Colors
Associated
with Leo

Leo's color is yellow, the brightest, warmest, sunniest and most radiant one, the color of the Sun at the zenith and of the self in all its power. This is a color that is difficult to attenuate; it captures and totally envelops one's glance, just like Leos attract others' attention. Yellow is a strong, virile color, the color of light and lift, symbolizing gold, luck and wealth. In China, it was the color of the emperor, in Persia of Mithras and in Greece of the solar god Apollo. In many religions, it is the color of the divine and of faith, as well as deceit and betrayal. Vishnu wears yellow garb and the cosmic egg of Brahma shines like gold. In the Islamic world, the color gold is the symbol of wisdom, while pale yellow stands for falsity. In Christian iconography, Judas is often represented with yellow clothing to indicate his betrayal. There is the yellow of sulfur and the yellow of eternal life: the symbolism of this color is two-fold, just as the Leo personality is never only light and, in fact, conceals hidden areas of shadow.

Add a touch of yellow in your home to enliven it, evoke light and warmth, as well as to transmit the energy this color radiates to those entering your home. Choose a golden yellow garment so that no obstacle will block your path, the relations and situations established during the day will be interwoven like gold thread. And, so that success and prosperity will come your way, as they do when you wear gold thread. You should wear an 'Egyptian yellow' garment (so called because it was a hue of yellow known by the ancient Egyptians and Assyrians) in order to increase your self-assurance and determination in a crucial moment. This is a color that makes even the slightest uncertainty disappear. Lastly, use lemon yellow if you want to exceed and provoke, astonish and fascinate, while pastel yellow should be worn when you have been excessively proud and presumptuous and when you must apologize and make up for a mistake.

Flowers
and Plants
Associated
with Leo

Leo marks the triumph of summer. The ears of wheat are ready to be reaped, the crickets sing, the Sun bestows its warmth, the whole world is a hymn to joy and prosperity. All the flowers that turn upward toward the Sun, such as sunflowers and heliotropes, are associated with Leo, as are the flowers that adore particularly sunny spots, such as the greater celandine (*Chelidonium Majus*) and gentian. Other flowers and plants whose color reminds one of the Sun are the yellow helichrysum, genista, tormentil (*Potentilla Tormentilla*), marigold and the saffron crocus (which, as its name implies, yields saffron), as well as juniper, laurel, lime, lemon and rosemary. The last-mentioned plant, in particular, should not be lacking in your diet and in your garden. In ancient times, rosemary was sacred to the Sun and the symbol of immortality and marital fidelity. It was thought able to ward off evil spirits and bad luck. Its branches and scent were especially potent talismans, and those who felt they had enemies made sure to have plenty of rosemary around them.

These are the flowers and the plants of the ten-day Leo periods:

First period (July 23-August 2): palm. The ancient Egyptians associated the palm tree with the goddess of love and joy, Hathor. The palm increases your power of seduction, and helps you, in affairs of love, to get to the point and clearly express your feelings.

Second period (August 3-13): rosemary. This aromatic herb is particularly precious for those born in this period. As a medieval saying states, "Those who wear the rosemary flower near the heart will always be merry and demons will flee from it." This plant is perfect to inspire a good mood, ward off bad influences of all kinds and help you sleep peacefully; furthermore, putting some rosemary leaves under your bed will protect you from bad dreams.

Third period (August 14-23): cyclamen. This is a humble, gentle flower that attenuates haughtiness and vain pride, to which Leos are prone every so often, and intensifies their sense of justice.

Animals Associated with Leo

The lion, the king of the animals and the symbol of noble vital energy and regal power, is the Leo animal par excellence. Just as the Sun is the king of sky, so this feline symbolizes sovereignty, power and authority. And, justice as well, since those who wield power must know how to govern and administer with equity. Figures of lions were sculpted on the throne of King Solomon, the French monarchs and the medieval prince-bishops. Leo has a strong sense of justice, loyalty and honesty. Leo's noble soul and rectitude are such that they can lead to sacrifice if necessary. The lion and all the other felines are, therefore, more than compatible with Leo's spirit. If Leo cannot have a tiger, panther, or ocelot to keep them company, a cat will do the trick. In fact, this is one of the animals suggested most for pet therapy, which is based on the interaction between humans and animals: stroking its fur is good for your pulse and blood pressure, and contact and company with a cat will cure depression, anxiety and solitude.

Leos are solar creatures and in a certain sense all animals that adore the Sun and its warmth can be associated with them: lizards in general, the green lizard and the scarab, which in ancient Egypt was the image of the Sun that is always resurrected, the symbol of the cycle of death and rebirth, eternal return. Again, other animals symbolically related to Leo are the rooster, which sings the praises of the rising Sun and personifies the strong character, boldness, and combativeness of the Leo personality, and the sparrow hawk, the bird of Horus, the solar emblem of the ancient Egyptians. The cricket, on the other hand, represents your generosity and prodigality, living in a carefree and extravagant manner, spending and squandering, and liberating your joyous energy without any control.

Gemstones Associated with Leo

Gold, the most noble and precious metal, "in which Helios' powerful breath makes those who possess it resplendent and most grave and solemn" (*Orphic Lapidary*), is quite compatible with those born under the Leo sign and emits positive vibrations. Leos should wear gold jewelry and stones such as amber, cat's eye and tiger's eye. Amber is a fossilized resin with a pleasant color that ranges from pale yellow to honey-yellow, orange, brown and reddish orange. In ancient times, physicians would pulverize it and mix it with honey or oils, then use it to cicatrize, lessen pain, and cure stomach ailments, headaches and toothaches. It was considered a powerful elixir, beneficial for all kinds of wounds and pains, except for the pangs of love. Amber is useful for remembrance, helping you to relive past moments with your lovers, thus maintaining the relationship and affection. Consequently, it should not be worn if you want to end a relationship that has come to its natural end. What you should do is to rub it in your hands if you want to activate a sort of protective shield, a field of energy that drives away everything negative. Cat's eye and tiger's eye are quartzes whose hues remind one of the iris of felines. They were once considered very powerful gemstones because it was thought they transmitted a sort of 'superior vision', the capacity to see beyond appearances, convenient truth or well concealed falsity. Just as felines can see at night, the person who wears these stones sees through the veil of the exterior and of illusory mirages. These gems should be worn if you do not want to make the wrong decision or a mistake, because both cat's eye and tiger's eye help you judge wisely. Again, if you have to deal with people who are hostile or mysterious, these gems will help you.

Best Food for Leo

Your solar sign is compatible with fire, flames, constant heat. But, unlike the lion of the savannah, you prefer well-cooked meat to raw meat, as well as beef, boar, duck and pigeon.

Leos are associated with strong, sour, piquant flavors and such fruit and vegetables as apricots, peaches, melons, watermelons, pepper, turnips, carrots, tomatoes, lettuce, squash and eggplant. Your menu should be the most varied and colorful possible, because at table, as in life, you love opulence, the sensation of well-being and merriment. But it should not be thought that Leos are demanding people who like only out of the ordinary food and tables laid for sumptuous banquets like those prepared in the court of Louis XIV, the Sun King. Although you do appreciate sophisticated or expensive food, you are more than satisfied if you see red tomatoes combined with yellow bell peppers and green zucchini on the table. You may love sumptuousness, but above all, you delight in chromatic opulence. The best spices to color and enliven your dishes are curcuma and saffron.

Associated with Leo are sudorific plants that, by increasing your body perspiration, contribute to the thermal regulation of your body and favor the elimination of toxins. Examples of these are borage, elder, linden, cinnamon, mint and above all chamomile, whose white petals and yellow corolla remind one of your heart, which is made of gold, and its candid ingenuousness. Known for its sedative and anti-inflammatory properties, chamomile was once harvested in bunches together with ripe wheatears. According to folk tradition, if this combination is placed on your doorstep it will propitiate wealth and keep poverty at a good distance. Lastly, your diet must include citrus fruit: lemons, grapefruit, lime, oranges, tangerines and Seville oranges.

Myths
Associated
with Leo

Leos are individualists and generous, proud and modest, daring and delicate, ingenuous and crafty, haughty and simple, authoritarian and permissive. This duality, this passionate, instinctive, feline nature that can also be tranquil, reasonable and reflective is mirrored in the mythical hero Heracles and the god Apollo, who represent two types of Leo: the Herculean and the Apollonian.

Heracles (Hercules in ancient Roman mythology) was the son of Zeus. His strength and prowess were legendary from the time he was a baby, and were so great that he strangled the two serpents that Hera had placed in his crib to kill him. This hero personifies the arrogant, self-assured, domineering person who lacks humility and must succeed in giving vent to his egoistic aggression, his dark side. Heracles has to do penance for killing his family in a fit of madness and is obliged to humbly serve King Eurystheus as punishment and perform twelve labors. The first was to kill the Nemean lion. These tremendous feats symbolize the painful and difficult quest for an equilibrium between instinct and reason, Leo's absolute need to dominate his own power, the tyrannical ego, and the tendency to unbridled exuberance.

Apollo, the solar divinity and god of art, music and prophecy, represents the Apollonian type, an idealistic Leo who, rather than dedicating his life only to imposing his will, to practical achievements and appearances, prefers artistic, creative, religious or ideological experiences. This is a Leo who decides to improve himself, develop and learn rather than satisfy his desires, is inspired and driven by joie di vivre as well as by a thirst for knowledge. This is a Leo who can accept defeat and learn from his mistakes, who is ready to get up and begin again after every fall.

While the Herculean type is realistic, vigorous, concentrates only on himself and led to dominate and impose himself, a prisoner of his ego, the Apollonian is an idealist connected to the luminous forces of the cosmos, with a strong, noble spirit.

Leo Fairy Tale

Aesop's fable *The Lion and the Mouse* embodies the spirit of Leo, the principle of strength, justice and dominion that expresses Leo's character.

The tale begins with a description of happy mice playing in the woods. One of them accidently falls on a lion that is sleeping. The king of the forest, irritated at being disturbed, captures the poor mouse and is about to eat it, but the poor creature begs him to be freed, promising that should the lion do so he will help him some day. This makes the lion roar with laughter: what could such an insignificant little mouse do for the majestic lion? In any case, he decides to let the mouse go free. Lo and behold, a few days later the mouse comes upon the lion, which has been trapped and tied with a rope by hunters. With its sharp teeth, the mouse cuts the rope and the lion can escape. Aesop suggests that we should not deride what we consider inferior, because even the weak can be of help to the strong.

Leos feel they are the best creatures of all, exemplifying and radiating self-confidence to the whole world. They do not feel the need to compete, do not question their strength or admit the possibility of needing other's help. But, the world is not always easy prey, is not always ready to praise them or submit to their every wish. Accepting the fact that they are not invincible, that they may lose a battle or two, and that cooperation and help from others are precious – all this is a truth that Leos must acknowledge and assimilate. Aesop's fable reveals another side of their character generosity, the tendency to protect rather than abuse the weak. The lion is the hero that those in difficulty can rely on. The weak derive strength and security from his energy, and those who are indecisive willingly let him lead them. It is in these moments, when the king is at the service of others, that the Leo personality acquires radiant splendor.

PATRIZIA TRONI, trained at the school of Marco Pesatori, writes the astrology columns for Italian magazines *Marie Claire* and *Telepiù*. She has worked in the most important astrology magazines (*Astra, Sirio, Astrella, Minima Astrologica*), she has edited and written the astrology supplement of *TV Sorrisi e Canzoni* and *Chi* for years, and she is an expert not only in contemporary astrology, but also in Arab and Renaissance astrology.

Photo Credits

Archivio White Star pages 28, 34, 38; artizarus/123RF page 20 center; Cihan Demirok/123RF pages 1, 2, 3, 4, 14, 30, 48; Yvette Fain/123RF page 46; file404/123RF page 16 bottom; Olexandr Kovernik/123RF page 42; Valerii Matviienko/123RF pages 8, 12; murphy81/Shutterstock page 44; Igor Nazarenko/123RF page 40; Michalis Panagiotidis/123RF pages 20, 21; tribalium123/123RF page 16; Maria Zaynullina/123RF page 36

WS White Star Publishers® is a registered trademark
property of De Agostini Libri S.p.A.

© 2015 De Agostini Libri S.p.A.
Via G. da Verrazano, 15 - 28100 Novara, Italy
www.whitestar.it - www.deagostini.it

Translation: Richard Pierce - Editing: Norman Gilligan

ISBN 978-88-544-0967-5
1 2 3 4 5 6   19 18 17 16 15

Printed in China